MW00795370

SHIFT

TO
AWAKEN AND
IGNITE
YOUR LIFE!

Dinavia Serro

Contents

This book is dedicated to Tiana, my angel and to

Keith, my eternal partner.

Acknowledgements

This book is finally here! I am beyond grateful for the editorial and publishing assistance I received to put this baby together...

I would like to thank Linda Carbone for stretching and pressing me to dig deeper, and helping my writing go to new places.

I would like to thank all the wonderful folks at Graham Publishing Group, who were involved with Shift to Awaken & Ignite Your Life.

Faith M., thank you for your brilliance and input. Your edits transformed my book incredibly. I'll be forever grateful for your patience and dedication to Shift.

Mr. Powerhouse Colin Graham, thank you for making this process seamless and smooth. You certainly hit the mark. Thank you for bringing my book to life!

My deepest appreciation goes to the reader of this book, I hope it resonates with you and helps add to your life in a positive way. This deep appreciation extends to those who are close and dear to my heart...

Mom, I did it!! I wrote the book that you always told me to write. Perhaps I'll send a copy to wherever you are up there – I love and miss you.

Saul, thank you for the start on this spiritual journey forty some odd years ago.

Art B., Donna and Keith, Maria R., Yoga Pura, MM – Thank you all for being in my life and adding to it in a special way.

My Hapuna Ohana on the Big Island, your incredible example of love, life and dedication changed my world in a profound way. Bess, Maka, Ginger & Julie. Mahalo! Aloha~

Nerdle McFly, Thank you for saving my life and bringing me life. I wouldn't be the grown up that I am today without you – You're incredible.

Dad, all that you have done was apparently enough. Here we are talking about the cosmos and solving life's mysteries. We are in the best place we've ever been! Love you.

Keith, An incredible journey it has been. You opened my world and showed me the world. Thank you for inspiring my life and cultivating an amazing ride. We are a great team. You're the smartest guy I've ever known! Love you.

Finally to my most precious and cherished of all – Tiana! You were and are the defining energy in my life. I'm incredibly secure with the person who you are. Your keen sense and ability to process is amazing, I'm proud of who you are. You're a good kid and the best daughter on the planet! Love you my angel~

Preface

There have been times in my life when I've asked, "Is this it? Is this what life is all about?" At other times, I've felt bland, bored, and frustrated with life. I needed something, anything, but at the time I had no clue what I needed. That was super frustrating! Come to find out, I wasn't the only one who felt that way. Many others I have connected with would share the same sentiments, only in different ways.

I have worked in the fitness industry for fifteen years as a certified personal trainer and fitness instructor. Interacting one-on-one with clients, as well as teaching group fitness classes, has given me insight into the human psyche and its many layers. I've seen motivation and drive in many forms, and also their exact opposite. After being witness to these behaviors over a period of time, I began to piece them together and found that they shared a common base: the mind, ego, and attachment.

I am also a certified yoga teacher and student of Eastern philosophies. This background has given me access to ancient texts and numerous publications on the subjects of Yoga, Buddhism, and Taoism. These studies provided me with many answers about why people adopt and act upon certain behaviors based on motivations or lack thereof.

Together these experiences led me to develop a platform of insight I could provide to both clients and other people I was engaged with. It includes glimpses of the inner workings of the mind and ego, and how they show up in daily life when making decisions. I used this platform to apply words and suggestions based on a person's situations and choices. I also explained how the mind and ego work in a way that people could understand and relate to. Irrespective of whom I shared this platform with, they were able to recognize their patterns and make changes to their lives for the better. It was, and still is, an effective means to the success of many. Sometimes when the perspective shifts, you obtain an opportunity to infuse change.

After presenting a fitness seminar in Hawaii a few years ago, I was approached by a few folks with questions regarding diet, exercise, and other health behaviors. As we spoke, I began to see a common thread: They all seemed to need answers that went beyond fitness and diet. I would answer their questions, and they would continue to talk about their needs, lack of motivation, dissatisfaction, confusion, and many other things.

All of these people were looking for life-changing information that I couldn't give them in a few minutes. I knew I had answers for them, and **SHIFT to Awaken and Ignite Your Life!** is my response to them and so many others who are looking for meaning and clarity amid the disappointments of modern life.

Here is what this book will do for you: It will give you the opportunity to live an enhanced and fulfilled existence by making the necessary changes in your life based on the insights, examples, and powerful suggestions that are provided within. It will also help you change defeating behaviors, repair and enhance personal relationships, eliminate a great deal of frustration, attain your goals, provide motivation, live life in a satisfying way, and give you overall life enhancement.

How can you enhance your life when you feel stressed and confused? Read on!

PART ONE

Perceptions and Beliefs: Taking a Look Within

~

Awaken Yourself to Life Enhancement, First Steps!

In order to access the path to enhancing your life, you need to take an honest look at how you live. How would you assess the overall quality of your life? What are some areas that are in need of change? Putting your life under a microscope can feel uncomfortable and even strange, or on the other hand, it can be exciting and refreshing, providing an interesting challenge. This forensic process automatically brings you the pinpoint accuracy you need to uncover, identify, and engage the keys to enhancing your life!

You must also understand and accept this key tenant: *Your experiences dictate your thoughts and opinions.* This is important because your thoughts and opinions in turn provide a backdrop and set a tone for your thinking and behavior. Your behavior and how you live out each day are in direct proportion to your perceptions and beliefs by way of the many *roles* you play every day.

Let's take a look several examples of what a perception/belief might be:

You Perceive		You Might Believe
Hard worker	⇨	This is how it must be done
Family oriented	⇨	Has to revolve around family
Busy	⇨	No time for anything
Overweight	⇨	You have to settle, frustrated
Old	⇨	Limited in some way
Fair	⇨	Limited expression of opinion, no boat rocking

Given the above list, you can see how perceptions are in direct proportion to beliefs. If you feel that you are busy and find yourself saying that often or using it as a go-to answer, for example, then this is a potential belief. As a result of the perception of busyness, the belief is there, ready to limit or perhaps eliminate other experiences from happening. Yes, there are times when you truly are busy and you may not have time to accommodate other things that may arise, but this example pertains to the habitual use of the term. So, having a perception that you are busy is in direct proportion to having a lack of time. The way you perceive something may establish a belief about it, and those beliefs set up a response based on that perception.

As you move through your day, how you respond to your interactions with people and situations is dependent on the role you are playing at the time and the perception and belief associated with that role. Let's take a deeper look at roles, their relationship to perceptions and beliefs, and how that can impact an interaction.

Roles and Interactions

Before you start your day, you probably don't think about the roles that you play during the day. You just go about business as usual, not really thinking about your social role of employee, parent, friend, sibling, cousin, spouse, etc. The dynamic in each of these roles is different, and you act accordingly. Sometimes these roles can overlap and layer, thereby leading to a less-authentic interaction.

Let's say your role as an employee demands that you oversee and manage a high-yielding department in sales. It takes a lot of hands-on work to govern a large group of people. The intensity of this role may spill over to a conversation or interaction you are having with a family member about party planning for a grandparent. Since you are already in the governing mode, you automatically assert your input as if it's the last word on the subject. You just react naturally as you would at work, so you think nothing of your response, but the family member has an entirely different feeling about it and takes umbrage to your input. As a result, energetically things start going downhill, nothing is decided or accomplished, nor does the family member state how unhappy she is. So this energy starts to build and branch out; it becomes the proverbial elephant in the room. This impacts your mood for the rest of your day in ways like being irritated and short with others and not enthusiastic about having to be somewhere or do something. The funny thing is, you probably don't even know what created this feeling to begin with, and you just continue on with a subpar day. All further interactions that day are tainted by the overlapping roles and lack of awareness of your actions, and hence the diminishing clarity and authenticity of those interactions.

Understanding that perceptions tie into beliefs and how that can impact an interaction is key to being aware of your actions! Life is dynamic and ever changing, so you can wear a number of hats. Some roles overlap and layer, which can create lack of clarity and authenticity during interactions. This can also impact your mood and tone for further interactions that day.

Let's look at another example of overlapping roles and how they impact a moment or a series of moments.

Sunglasses!

Eric Walrabenstein, a cherished teacher of mine, provides another example:

"Let's say that a perception/belief represents one pair of sunglasses that I have in front of me, and I have eight pairs. I put on one pair, and the room gets darker. I then put on the second pair, and it's even darker. The third pair goes on, and I can't see the chair in front of me. The fourth: I can barely make out that my hand is in front of my face! For every pair of glasses I put on, my vision gets impaired and my ability to react and be fully aware is hindered."

Your awareness is impaired by layers and overlapping roles. Sometimes when you have an image or a situation (like the sunglasses) to define a concept, understanding that concept can become easier. Regarding this subject of overlapping roles and their effects, you have to first identify what it is that needs to be sorted out in order to start removing the layers. You can do that by first recognizing your patterns.

Patterns

You may have a pattern for every role you play in your life and every role you play in your day. Once a pattern is established, you can get used to it, and not only does it become part of your life but it also may dictate how you live your life. So, just imagine how many established patterns you have that are dictating how you live your life. Seeing how perceptions and roles can directly affect your happiness and fulfillment levels every day gives you the ability to think about your choices and what actions (if any) you will take based on those choices.

Earlier I used the example of an interaction between family members and how the choice of words (or lack thereof) resulted in a not-so-stellar outcome. Now let's say the sales manager had the *awareness* to not insert her work role into the decision process for the grandparent's party and also recognized how her perception of herself being a boss/manager could directly affect the tone of the interaction with the other family member. The result would have been drastically different. Instead of both parties feeling uneasy or upset about the interaction, they would be happy and satisfied with the outcome. The sales manager would take the opportunity to think about the potential negative outcome of the interaction and through this make a choice to respond differently with her choice of words. By being aware of perceptions, patterns, and roles, the sales manager could take a different approach to the response.

This is all about making choices that serve your highest and greatest good. Over time, once you honor the opportunity to become present, your instincts will become sharpened and you'll make better decisions. Until that becomes manifest, it's like anything else in life: We take what we like or need and leave the rest, or just end up settling for what is in front of us.

Sometimes settling doesn't give you what you need and creates further disintegration of your awareness. Your ability to respond clearly while interacting with others or responding to everyday life diminishes with every layer of influence you carry over from other roles in your day. Having the ability to identify how this occurs, and taking action to change it, is a giant step toward living a peaceful existence. If you happen to settle for a behavior and the actions associated with it fully knowing that you are not existing in a quality situation because of it, you limited your ability to make choices that serve your greatest good, as well as not taking appropriate action to change the situation. This is how disintegration of your awareness is perpetuated!

Become aware of your inhalations and exhalations, feel your heartbeat, or notice how the wind rustles through the trees. Dial into what is going on rather than being on autopilot. Any of these actions can provide the type of focus you need to identify the influences you carry over from other behaviors. As it relates to patterns and responses, your awareness can be that of recognizing and witnessing how you behave within a role and the responses you generate by being in that role. Once you've identified a certain pathology that exists within a pattern and begin to change elements of it through elimination and redirection to serve your highest needs, you are on your way to living and interacting authentically.

This change can be implemented in steps. As an example, let's say you have a less-than-stellar dynamic of interaction with a family member and you both usually end up talking over each other. When sharing an important thought or topic with this person, she somehow seems to make it about herself and fails to acknowledge your feelings or give you the understanding that you need. This results in you challenging her response by addressing her self-centered behavior. Trigger! This is the pathology of this relationship.

You can take the initial step of change by removing the expectation that the situation should be anything other than what it is. Don't share deeper topics with this individual, because you already know the possible outcome. Don't respond as you normally would to this person. You *already* know the dynamic of the interaction if you do respond normally, so why not try holding your urge to shoot back and say almost nothing in a neutral way? These are a few ways to begin changing and making choices that serve your greatest good. Over time, you will begin to experience increased quality with everyone you interact with because of your integrated approach of awareness, implementation, and change.

Your perceptions and beliefs are an important part of your life. Recognizing what they are can help you navigate through life more successfully. There may be some who are content with their perceptions and beliefs, and I say to them cheers and bravo! Those individuals have eluded the *needs and desires* that plagues most of us. The rest of us have an insatiable need to be fulfilled, putting us on an endless search outside of ourselves for this fulfillment.

By examining your perceptions and beliefs, you will clearly see where you have room to make adjustments. Recognizing patterns is a part of this forensic process.

Cow Paths

Have you ever seen a cattle or cow path? Constant use has worn a clearly defined path. The cows do not deviate from that path. That is the way they choose to get wherever they are going.

With every pattern there is a role, and for every role there is a pattern. The paths you take in life are usually carved according to the role you are playing and the pattern that role requires. It's an automatic response or go-to pattern that has been established in your wiring system. Imagine that everything that occurs in your life takes place within a box. No matter what the situation or occurrence, you bounce off the same four walls. The results are going to be limited to the capacity of the box: same four walls, same set of outcomes.

People whose lives are *stuck in a rut* are living this kind of limited, repeating pattern. The driving force behind it is the cumulative effect of having a disintegrative awareness. In effect, being layered and overloaded with responses and behaviors creates distractions that hinder one's ability to see a different picture. Dulling your ability to respond to phenomena to gain your best possible outcome is an example of disintegrative awareness. Another reason for this rut could be the settling aspect that I mentioned earlier; this is a condition of going along with what is happening, even though you know it is not the best for you to do so. Over time, this can make you feel stuck and limited, frustrated, empty, and seeking some sort of resolution. If no resolution appears, the outcome may be settling for life in that state. Why would anyone do that?

I have an idea why; let's take a look at humans "being."

The Mind, Ego, and Comfort

As humans, we are creatures of comfort. We like comfy couches, pillows, food, and situations. We like all these things because of their EASE. They require no difficulty or effort; they're simple, gentle.

If you think about it, to create a new cow path would require work, effort, and some difficulty over time. It's easy to stick with the status quo, to just do what you normally do. This requires no change and is somewhat automatic and comfortable. Whenever you venture into an unknown space, it may cause some discomfort because you've never experienced it before, you don't have any data, and you don't know what to expect. This perception of discomfort or comfort is driven by the ego.

In a nutshell, the ego represents the aspect of you that identifies as "I" or "me." It basically dominates actions and choices that revolve around satisfying the self.

The ego will continue to seek and fulfill based on its need for satisfaction. Let's use the example of being in *ease and comfort* mode, which requires no work. Compare that to the work needed to create a new cow path to lead those cows to a new pasture that fulfills their need for space, abundant food, and shelter. Even though the new pasture provides the promise of abundance, peace, and ease (once the cows are settled and established), many will still take the old path, remaining in *ease and comfort* mode. An example of the ego choosing comfort is seeing toned, lean, and fit bodies and wanting to look that amazing, but not being willing to do the work required achieve it. Some people understand the negative effects of smoking and the great life-changing benefit they would receive if they stopped, but that still isn't enough to institute change. It takes too much effort and work to get there.

The ego is attached to the routine and outcomes it has established over time, so it remains on a repetitive journey. Now let's apply the opposite of ease and comfort as it pertains to the ego and how it functions. It's important to see many aspects of this multifaceted psyche that we come equipped with at birth. The ego can also root itself in hard work (whatever you define hard work to be) as well. It indulges in behaviors that represent repetitiveness, familiarity, and staid processes in order to maintain its existence and satisfaction. The behaviors could be of comfort, hard work, or doing absolutely nothing! Whatever the ego identifies with is what it feeds off. It further sees itself as the "I" or "me" with every repeated behavior. This is limiting, because that's all that you end up experiencing.

Working, taking action, or busying oneself is often attached to a goal, whether it's obtaining money, distraction, or feeling needed in some capacity. That too is the ego's playground.

Before you read on, take a moment to write down in list form how certain actions or activities can be a playground for the ego. You might jot down things like:

• Working long hours
• Sitting on the couch knowing other things have to get done
• Getting wrapped up in physical appearance and always trying to obtain a look
• Being a super volunteer who does everything

These are a few examples of what your list might look like. You can draw from examples in your own life, or even what you witness in friends and co-workers. A template is provided on the following page to jot down this *Ego Candy*.

Ego Candy

_____

_____

_____

_____

_____

_____

_____

_____

_____

No Satisfaction

The ego is rooted in "I," "me," and "need," and constantly searches to be fulfilled. If it happens to find this fulfillment through work or effort, it will continue that behavior. If it finds that hard work is the most gratifying outcome, it will continue to do that. Ego will use certain thoughts, actions, or words that provide these feelings as well. Let me put it this way: Ego will burn a path and burn it some more if it's being satisfied. But guess what? *It is never satisfied!*

Although ego may be receiving what it needs from its current path, it always wants more. Have you ever heard people say they'll be happy **when** they get a new car or **when** they go on vacation? Well, they get the car or the vacation and that excitement fades. It was attached to some happiness condition, so it fades along with the excitement about the object of their desire.

Recognizing how this works and how it can affect your daily life is important. Remaining in a steady state of awareness of your actions and how those actions impact your life can make a big difference in how you choose to live. This steady state can prevent the uneven perceptions of being happy-happy then feeling low-low based on the ego's need for conditional attachments. Even the perceptions of how you "should be" according to the roles you play have to be met with the vigilance of a disciplined mind.

The ego will even resist the chance to *see* something differently. I mention this because there may be a point along this journey when you say, "Why am I doing this? This is all too much effort!" If this happens, I want you to understand why it is happening. This will take some effort, consistency, and discipline, but once these processes are implemented, you will reap the reward from the personal efforts you put forth to produce this change in your daily life. Over time, as you create new pathways, your life will become more fulfilled and *enhanced*! Clarity is the name of the game; having a clear mind as you approach things and having an understanding of why you are doing what you do equate to awareness. Awareness = Clarity.

We, in a society filled with technology and advancements, want things NOW. That conditioning is the result of our culture bombarding us with endless options to fulfill our desires. If you want food, just drive up to a window at *any time* day or night and you will have food! You want more options, go to Costco, Target, or wherever else—there will be more than plenty to go around. The mighty internet gives immediate gratification as well—does this satisfy the ego or what?!? You can see how this has conditioned your thinking and actions to expect things immediately—yet another potential pattern that plays a role in your daily life and adds several pairs of sunglasses as well!

This ego-driven behavior, coupled with your many pairs of sunglasses, leave you with a disconnected, fragmented, unfulfilled, and confusing existence that limits your ability to live an enhanced life. Living with clarity in your choices and interactions by eliminating conditioned thinking and responses from repetitive behaviors is an example of living an enhanced life. When you have the freedom to live and react without a built-in template, your life becomes enhanced. This is more than enough reason to create an authentic space for existing. By eliminating conditioned responses, you now have room to acknowledge your true feelings and needs. Allowing you to process and experience yourself in a new way, this will ultimately lead you to your authentic space of existing. Finding that authentic space requires:

Awakening

• Identifying your patterns and removing your sunglasses one by one

• Taking a fearless inventory of what you have in excess and don't need

Igniting

• Recognizing repetitive paths

• Meeting things evenly, being in a steady state of awareness

• Staying not too high, not too low

• Expending effort, consistency, and discipline

• Spending *at least* 5 to 10 minutes a day in complete silence, closing your eyes and tuning out mind chatter and all else

New Pathways

"You are your synapses. They are who you are."
—Joseph Le Doux, Synaptic Self, 2002

In the last chapters, you learned how your patterns and beliefs can affect your behaviors and how you go about your life. This awareness leaves the door open for change by creating new pathways for you to experience your life in a brand-new existence.

That sounds super fantastic, right? So how do you obtain and experience this fantabulous existence? Well, I have an answer—a few, in fact.

Before we get into the ways you can obtain this existence, let's take a look at the big impact our brain has on this process and how its physiological response can assist or inhibit your outcome. I will try to make this as simple as possible.

Here goes:

Your central nervous system signals the brain based on thought, something visual, visceral stimuli, ego preferences ↧

↧ Brain receives electrical impulse (charge)

↧ Activates neurotransmitters

↧ Neurotransmitters bind with receptors

↧ Action potential is created (synapse function)

↧ "Action" message sent

Behavior results

Often a synapse function creates a hardwired response, and your ability to exist consciously takes a backseat to an automatic response of repetitive thoughts, actions, and behaviors. Over time, this autopilot makes up who you are personality-wise—and that may or may not be who you are to the world or who you want to be. Joe Dispenza sums this up nicely: *"We are producing the same mind on a daily basis because we are firing the same neural networks in the same routine patterns, combinations and sequences."*

Making a conscious effort to be aware of your behaviors and patterns, you can start to identify and pinpoint the areas that don't serve you fully, or where you feel you are not living authentically. This awareness is all you need for your next brain adventure . . . creating new synapse functions!

With focused attention, you can start to really change the hardwired responses from your brain. By associating your desire to create or change a behavior with the conscious application of consistency and repetition, you will produce a chemical response in the brain that over time will create a new neural network with fresh-out-of-the-package synapse functions.

You can be ever changing, ever evolving, if you understand and have knowledge of the power that you are capable of. Harnessing that power is the key. It takes true desire and effort to succeed.

"By neurochemically encoding repeated events through the mastery of knowledge and experience, we will genetically become what we mastered," explains Joe Dispenza.

Remember that the ego wants to convenience itself, so it will repeat preferable pathways to obtain this, even if it's on a constant loop.

Now that you have a glimpse at how the ego works and how it could possibly interrupt this process of creating a new neural net, you also have an idea of what to look out for and what to move past in order for this process to take place. Let me hit you with one more thing, since we're on the subject.

This new neural network or new synapse can get old and become something that no longer serves you over time. Just as patterns and behaviors become less helpful in our lives, the chemical responses in the brain that created them may need an upgrade or a change as well. As I stated earlier, you are ever changing and dynamic, and the platforms you use are also dynamic. That is one of the great things about being alive: the ability to adapt and change!

And This Is How You Do It!

I suggest keeping a journal or notebook that will hold the ongoing lists and exercises you'll be doing, or you can use the templates I've provided. They will cover your insights, awareness, and, at times, records of your unconscious communicating to you *authentically*. They are yours and should be highly respected!

The exercises in the following pages are incredibly powerful and transformational. The transformation happens with every pen stroke, honest acknowledgment, and discerning look within. Be fearless with your journey and process, for you are your own warrior on this mission to peace, ease, and self-awareness.

One exercise will have you extract information from some uncovered places within and perform an engaged writing task in list form. Another is a conscious application of spontaneity. The third exercise involves your proactive input in ego behavior identification. This exercise will really take you out of a complacent space of consciousness into a dynamic, interactive, and empowering existence.

Perceptions and Beliefs Exercise

Make a list of your top ten perceptions and beliefs, then next to each one write a few words to describe the reason you hold that perception or belief. In the first column, write the perception or belief; in the second, record the reason you hold that perception or belief; and, finally, in the third say what you'd rather be doing or what you wish your life was like. An example looks something like this:

Perceptions & Beliefs		Reasons	Wish I . . .
Old	⇨	Feeling limited	Had more energy, felt inspired, and took better care of myself.
Busy	⇨	Not enough time	Made more time to do what I want to do!
Fair	⇨	Don't want to rock the boat	Considered my needs and myself.

This is a big exercise, and it may come easily and quickly, or it may take some time for you to formulate what it is that you are feeling. If you're feeling like you are in a rut and are uninspired, for example, you could list what that feels like physically in your body. Are you feeling like you need to exercise? Do you feel weighted down? If so, then jot down what you are feeling in your body. Now jot down how you feel mentally—is there a block of creativity? Are you bored? Or if there is anything else that comes up, jot it down. That is the best way to formulate your feelings. As I stated earlier, it may take a quick moment to determine or you may need time to think about or get in touch with your feelings. Be patient with yourself, and your answers will come loud and strong. You will feel them, and once you do, this is a gateway for you to express what has been repressed. What is being accomplished on these sheets of paper is that you are consciously giving direct attention to your behaviors based on your beliefs and perceptions, as well as bringing to life and giving rise to your dormant needs, dreams, and ideas.

Perceptions & Beliefs		Reasons	Wish I . . .
	⇨		
	⇨		
	⇨		
	⇨		
	⇨		
	⇨		

As you move through this exercise, you are uncovering, peeling away, or removing many pairs of sunglasses! This will allow you to gain clarity on your perceptions and beliefs. You only listed your top ten beliefs and perceptions, but life is dynamic, in constant movement. It may require *many* lists as you go along, allowing you to navigate your day and your life from a clear and authentic perspective. Whenever there is a purging of sorts, you feel lighter. It can be cleaning out a junk drawer or getting rid of items in your closets. The end result is that you feel uncluttered and free. You can actually feel the space become less dense and lighter. The same concept goes for this exercise: As you purge and rid yourself through this uncovering process, you will feel lighter and unencumbered. This is the fluidity that will allow your awareness and your clarity to be sharp in order to see your behaviors and motivations.

Identifying and becoming aware of your own perceptions and beliefs is incredibly powerful, because it causes you to become directly connected to your behaviors consciously. Being conscious of what, how, and why will bring the knowledge to inspire change and growth that is needed to exist with a perspective of who you are and what you need authentically.

Right now, the list may only be ten or fewer items, and that is perfect because you need to work individually with what is written on that paper. As you go through line by line, peeling away your true feelings about the subject, you will gain a clear understanding about what, how, and why specific to that particular line item. If there are several line items, you will have to allow the proper time to navigate through them in order to get to the bottom line. That is the act of the *purge*. It's powerful and transformational, and you will feel it!

As life goes on, you'll create new lists, and you will go through your process of identification in order to get rid of what is no longer serving you. This now is ongoing and is your sacred journal that you can go to for answers. Everything contained within is authentic and created by you. You've created your own reference material about yourself, and you can see your growth and how your perspective has shifted. This may be useful as you go along on your life journey.

The Phenomenon of Spontaneity Exercise

Once you depart from your "normal" patterns and actions, there is room for spontaneity and movement. When we experience spontaneity, it's nonrestrictive, and in most cases it sparks enjoyment and excitement! This is what we are going for: the spark that ignites excitement and joy. This can bring fulfillment into your day! This is an important tool in your quest for life enhancement.

Allowing an event to unfold and experiencing it without a lens or sunglasses can be uplifting and new. Here are some ideas that you can apply to use spontaneity in your own life:

• Take a different route home if possible. Try carpooling.

• Paint a room in your home a different color.

• Make meals from a cookbook several times a week.

• Change your perfume or cologne.

- Clean out a junk drawer and fill it with something cool (like money or photographs).
- Change your hairstyle.
- Give flowers to someone you cherish and respect.
- Go out dancing or dance at home!
- Wear a color you have never worn.
- Go on vacay or staycay.
- If it's possible, sleep outside for a night in a tent.

OK, sleeping outside for a night in a tent probably doesn't equate to a major life change, but what it DOES provide is a change of routine, and possibly a new way to see yourself exist. Do you know how you exist sleeping in a tent? How would you navigate that? You wouldn't know it unless you've experienced it. So, if camping is your norm, then please bypass this suggestion! If not, give it a shot and try it. See yourself interact in a situation that is not your norm.

The things on this list are not (within themselves) life changers, but what they are is a means to express, exist, and *be* in another way spontaneously. By implementing these little changes or actions, you are creating new ways to process an experience.

These are just some ideas to do things a little differently, so you can get another experience and perspective. By taking these small, spontaneous actions and actively finding ways of living authentically, your awareness and attention to your life will increase considerably. Once you are equipped with the knowledge you have gained through your fearless efforts, you will be "in the know" and you can never go back to the place of not having this knowledge. This in turn will keep you moving forward on the momentum you have created for yourself. Creation is unlimited and infinite. Your ability to think and create doesn't have a time limit; it is unlimited and not bound by time. Your imagination and creativity are a stream of consciousness. Have you ever been immersed in something and you lose track of time? Well, this is like that. The ideas and creativity you express are without time, they're unlimited. You can tap in and be on that path in an instant. You can continue to craft your existence as you see fit, whenever it needs change.

There are ways to eliminate the routinized patterns you create for yourself, if that is your choice. It starts with identifying and questioning your patterns and roles. Seeing where the ego has a stronghold or a role in the cycle can help identify the stagnation or lack of creating something new in your life.

Knowing how to access contentment in your life leads to a life lived fully, and that is what I wish for all of us on this planet.

Ego Behavior Identification (EBI) Exercise

In "The Mind, Ego, and Comfort" section, I asked you to write down how taking action and busying yourself could be a playground for the ego. I had you make a list of examples (either personal or otherwise) that provide gratification, or "candy," for the ego.

Congratulations on writing those lists. They are a BIG step toward your heightened awareness! It may have seemed like an unassuming thing to do, but you had to go deep into areas of your psyche to extract information that is true and authentic. It came from the true persona and essence of who you are without sunglasses, roles, perceptions, or beliefs. This space within doesn't get accessed that often because we are generally surface players.

By virtue of writing those lists (and breaking the surface) and taking the journey within, you gave yourself a powerful tool that you can use as an oracle of sorts to see what to look out for, or just to have some helpful insight.

Let's say you happen to display or experience a behavior that reflects something on your list. You can immediately change course by:

- Identifying the behavior
- Modifying or ceasing the behavior
- Noting why the behavior is occurring!

By identifying a specific behavior, you are narrowing the playing field to one thing specifically, then you are able to make changes to modify it or stop it altogether. It is also important to recognize why or what caused the behavior, because then you'll know what to avoid in order not to repeat it.

> "What is necessary to change a person is to change his awareness of himself." —Abraham Maslow

Identify

First you must identify behaviors you engage in automatically or unconsciously. This requires observing your own behavior, which is a necessary step toward bringing something to a conscious level in order to recognize its impact and take action to modify it, if necessary. Being alert to behaviors that you perform automatically or unconsciously puts you on a definite path to self-awareness, which will bring clarity and balance to your life.

Food is a good example to show the concept of awareness and lack thereof. Sometimes what motivates a person to consume food is the need to feel security or to fix things emotionally. In order to fill that void and cover the emotions, you may reach for food, alcohol, or whatever else. You usually do this impulsively, and it often results in overconsumption. Over time, you are still eating and filling, but you're also feeling the same emotionally—nothing has changed. Until the underlying reason for the compulsion is identified, the pathology will remain the same. If you are alerted to the root causes, awareness happens and hopefully healing begins in order for you to exist in life with clarity and balance.

By identifying, modifying, or ceasing the behavior and noting why the behavior is occurring, you can address things within yourself that you feel need to be shifted. Even if it's something that comes up during the day that you just don't feel right about and is creating inner conflict, stop and take a moment to identify what that is, then find a way to change it or rid yourself of it. It is also important to try to figure out how it came about in the first place, because you probably don't want to repeat it. Your goal is to be in tune with yourself and what you are feeling, as well as allowing your mind the time to process things.

Engage

Once equipped with the ability to self-study, you can operate from a different perspective by shifting your gears to an engaged and alert setting. This will allow the process of change to occur in the areas that have been highlighted during the uncovering and identifying portion of the EBI. This knowledge is yours; use it to empower yourself to make the modifications you need to create the way you want to live. The process of becoming engaged will enable you to *Awaken*, and you should write it down in that journal or notebook of yours. As a result, you'll have notes on the attributes of your experience to reflect on, if necessary.

Notes on the Exercises

All three of the above exercises are designed to uncover, identify, and engage. They aren't designed to be done all at once, as each may require a little more or less of your time and input to extract information. Every exercise should be a well thought-out and felt process to allow the thoughts to flow. It is key for your work to resonate from authenticity, no matter what!

Tapping into those areas within that lie dormant and creating new synapse functions and different ways of processing to enhance life is courageous! You are on your way to an exciting, unknown adventure that will bring you to YOU!

The Importance of Your Written Responses

Sacred texts, including the Bible, are highly respected and held at a high level of vibration. Since many people hold the Bible or any other religious or sacred texts in high regard, there is an energy that is created around them merely by the thoughts generated about them. Here's another way to think about a high level of vibration: Have you ever been to a concert or a pep rally? The energy generated is usually quite high, and everyone is tuned in to the same focus. This is what makes the place hum and vibrate with an uplifting effect. The collective of people all focused on the same subject and intent in an uplifting way also raises the vibration within the space and of the performer or speaker as well. Thoughts are energy. Guess what? Your journal or notebook is that type of vibration too, and should be regarded as such. Just as folks turn pages in the Bible to seek some insight or answer, you will find that answer within your journal or notebook as well. Not only will you see the answer, you will have CREATED it yourself. That's harnessing your own power!

Personal Notes

PART TWO

The Bottom-Line Articles

Compositions To Inspire New Thoughts And Personal Investigation

Part Two of this book was written to encourage and introduce another way of thinking about things, to possibly create a shift of your awareness toward how you view life in everyday scenarios and circumstances, and also how that view could be transformed in order to create an enhanced way of existing!

In Part One of this book, you read about the ego, how it functions, and how roles and behaviors impact your life. In the following pages, you will see through thought-provoking stories and scenarios how the essence of the ego, roles, and behaviors infuse themselves into situations and circumstances. As such, these articles offer another way for you to gain a larger understanding of how the mind exists and works. They also provide you with inspiration to shift your current thought process, thereby creating new synapse functions in your brain and ultimately a new pathway of thought to bounce off.

Following each reading, you will be asked a question about the content, how you relate to it, what your feelings are around it, and whether you have had a related experience. By answering these questions, you are uncovering and illuminating areas of your mind that will draw you further toward where your true essence and feelings reside. Your responses should go into the journal or notebook that you used in Part One, or on the provided templates.

Get ready for another journey toward your true self . . .

Cattle and Cookie-Cutter Existence

I once lived in a master planned community. Being in that environment gave me the opportunity to experience the collective consciousness of that specific setting. It also provided me with a look into our culture as a collective, and how we are spoon-fed in a consumer-based, big-box retail society, to say the least.

It came as no surprise to see how a master planned community would fit right in with our society's constant message of "bigger is better" and "get more, be more." Keeping up with the Joneses isn't a joke in this particular master planned environment; some folks are truly trying to one-up their neighbors in ways that are important to them and also in ways that represent their class. I guess one of the reasons for this is that when you have sprawling acres of tract homes devoid of originality, hinting of everything "Stepford" and uniform, you may just need to identify yourself differently from your neighbors. This can manifest itself through curb appeal with a sprawling green lawn, a man cave, cool garage, or having all of the latest and greatest home gadgets, car, etc. . . .

In respect to socially identifying with "more," parents vie for positions within their respective circles in schools and organizations. Parents having intense passion for and participation in their child's sports and showing that in every way they can, by becoming a team parent, contributing financially, or otherwise. Again, in the essence of society's message of "bigger is better," these actions of exposing and representing oneself in these circles and in particular ways touches upon this need to be and to feel like "I'm the best," or something of that nature. That being said, **some** parents (NOT ALL) involve themselves with school functions, sports activities, and various other organizations just to exercise their need to feel important.

Being that our society has placed overriding emphasis on bigger, better, and best, it's no wonder that this competitive behavior is displayed and is in a constant loop! Due to this overbearing inundation (as a collective), we have forgotten and ignored the individual quality and truth that resides within all of us. We are equipped with intuition and creativity that gets watered down with repetitive actions or behaviors that fill our lives.

This limited way of existing is due in part to the already cued up, ready-to-go cookie-cutter templates we use to respond at that given time. So let's say you have a situation that is in direct relation to competitiveness. Your template of response for that mode will be cued up and used. Having these automatic go-tos eliminates your ability to create and use your critical thinking authentically on the fly. The term "I just do what I've always done" comes to mind. Remember the discussion of the cow path? Not very different, huh?

Questions to Ponder:

Can you identify a cookie-cutter response that you may have on a constant loop to an aspect of your life?

_____

_____

_____

_____

What ways would you create a new way of responding?

_____

_____

_____

_____

Do you feel the need at times to be viewed a certain way socially?

If so, can you analyze why you feel that way? What steps would you take to change that response, if necessary?

_____

_____

_____

_____

By identifying this loop, you can see if it's something that needs to be there. Does it serve you in any way? Is it more of a hindrance? The answers that you provide to these questions will help you identify and eliminate what you feel needs to go.

Creating new ways of responding gives you a new way of expressing yourself so you can get out of the repeated pattern.

"Every time you are tempted to react in the same old way, ask if you want to be a prisoner of the past or a pioneer of the future." —Deepak Chopra

Looking at why you need to be viewed a certain way socially can identify something that needs to be met on a deeper level. Staying with the example of "I'm the best" from the above reading, this could possibly indicate not feeling valued, or feeling that you're not enough. This can show up in a social setting as a person overdoing things or placing an importance on their value through financial contribution or time spent on a particular venture.

By taking a look at this need, you can change attributes that you no longer feel a connection to, and also see if this is a staid response from your template mode.

Just Push Play

One size does not fit all.

It is common for people to greet each other with the phrase "How are you?" or "How's your day going?" But do we really listen to the response to these questions? Do we really care about the answers? Personally, I find that this greeting (and the response that usually follows) is often empty and devoid of any true feeling. In effect, we are just following a routine that has been hardwired into our neural circuits. You might as well just push "play" on a tape recorder, since you say or ask the same thing over and over. Have you ever thought about this interaction?

Granted, greeting people probably rates low on the scale of importance. However, what if you made eye contact and showed true interest when you greeted another person? What if you actually listened to the response rather than signing off as soon as you asked the question? Perhaps a smile would impact that moment far more than an empty, meaningless question does. What makes it meaningless is the whole way the interaction is handled. What if there were a different approach? For example, let's take a routine task like checking out at a market. Would the quality of the interaction change if you were to truly engage with the person scanning your groceries by making eye contact as you greeted him, then really listened to his response, with real interest? The person with whom you are engaging would then see and feel that you are giving him your undivided attention. This appreciation instantly brings quality and meaning to the whole interaction! Have you ever given someone a gift, and in doing so, it made you feel really good? Well, in essence, when you engage with someone as I have just described you're giving the gift of your attention and focus. If you link enough of these magical moments together every day, you will transform your life with peace, ease, and incredible heart happiness.

I understand that sometimes you just don't want to be bothered and want to tune out—we all have those days—but the message here is to try to become conscious of your actions. Develop the ability to raise awareness in your life, because it is so easy to follow a routine path. Heck, we do it every day! Our daily life is somewhat scripted, and a by-product is that our thought process takes a backseat, hence we become complacent and use the same tape repeatedly (just push "play"). Have you ever noticed the condition of an arena or theater after a sporting event or movie? Often there is garbage all around. Some leave trash behind because (a) they think someone else will clean it up, (b) everybody else does it, or (c) laziness. This is just one example of the mind succumbing to routine and the complacent nature that is reflective of our society's collective consciousness. So, if we try to recognize and see what has become invisible to us through desensitization and ignorance, I believe that we can raise our individual awareness. Now, if we all did that, well . . . we shall see!

"The miracle is not to walk on water. The miracle is to walk on the green earth, dwelling deeply in the present moment and feeling truly alive." —Thich Nhat Hanh

I was fortunate enough to attend one of the best yoga teacher training programs in the country, at Yoga Pura in Phoenix, Arizona. During this intense yearlong process, we were exposed to and taught many valuable lessons about yoga, yoga philosophy, and life. At one of these dynamic sessions, Eric Walrabenstein explained the concept of "getting all the way in the water." He encouraged us to engage fully and give 100 percent of our attention to whatever we are doing at that moment, whether it be engaging in an interaction, performing an activity, or even sitting idly. By virtue of this saturation, you get all aspects and facets, and you experience the whole thing.

Questions to Ponder:

How can this be applied to other areas in your life?

_____

_____

_____

_____

Can this apply not only to the routine but to the true nuts and bolts of your existence? If so, how?

_____

_____

_____

_____

If you can pinpoint where you are delivering routinized responses in your life, it can open up a variety of aspects of yourself that you may not know you have! The outcome of engaging someone who is providing a service, such as checker at a grocery store, could possibly fill your heart with the kindness that is shared through words and making eye contact. This in turn can affect your mood for the rest of your day. That is just one way to see how applying awareness and engagement to whatever it is you are doing can make you mindful of the moments you are in.

To apply this process to how you exist, you would see if the way you're existing is the way you want to be, and examine how you arrived where you are. You can ask yourself if the decisions that you made to get you to this place were made with a true desire.

For example, if you've settled for anything in your life such as a relationship, career, or anything else, this decision has shaped your existence and how you live, respond, and relate to some extent. It's safe to say that the engagement level of that decision was not at its full capacity because you ended up settling for what was in front of you. If you're longing for a change or need to release an aspect of your life based on past decisions, list what you feel you need to address so you can work on making changes to it. You'll make this list from an awoken state. Being aware of what your current needs are and how they can be fulfilled then acting on them is key to having enhanced existence. You will no longer be settling, but will be empowered to live the life you deserve to live.

Heat and Intensity!

A volcano erupting, a rupture in the planet's crust spewing lava and making new land formations is a wonderful spectacle of nature. It's a building-up process of intensity that explodes and creates anew! How powerful is that?

With heat comes a certain intensity. Maintaining a high level of output over a period of time creates intensity too. Sometimes this intensity can be viewed in a negative fashion if it applies to our lives by way of situations or people considered overbearing and heavy. Intensity can also be seen as a means of volition, self-expression, drive, and constancy. I describe intensity as (1) where satisfaction and urgency merge, (2) the need to have something met on a deep level and hold its energy to completion, (3) opposing levels at the same frequency, like magnets creating a static contraction until they meet. Heat and intensity happen in everyday life as well as in nature, and we can learn a great deal from nature by refamiliarizing ourselves with its magnificent processes.

Think back to a time in your life when you faced a difficult situation, a really tough time that you thought would never end and had you in a major spin. Now, looking back, you see the meaning, the gem, and appreciate the true magic of it because without it, you would not be where you are right now in life. I can share a personal experience that serves as a good example of this. Back in 2008, my husband had a medical emergency that completely changed our lives. The series of events that followed led us down an unknown path filled with fear, doubt, vulnerability, fulfillment, and ultimately success.

At the time, it was difficult to extract the gem and recognize the transformational nature that the situation was providing to us because we were in the thick of it. After things settled and time passed, we became aware of the many gifts the medical emergency brought to us. For instance, it became very evident to us how precious life is and what's really important relative to our lives together, so much so that we decided to move to another state and live our lives exactly the way we wanted to. We also chose to focus on our moments together and how much we appreciated each other as a family unit. We attained a level of quality that was never there before, and we couldn't imagine living life without having it. That was the gem, the gift that we experienced from our difficult situation.

Through the process of high pressure, extreme heat, and intensity, a diamond is formed.

Tha's how powerfully transformational that situation was; the intense nature of it made it transformational. Not all difficult situations carry the same energy. Some of them are just there to transform your life. The magic of the transformation is what I am trying to explain and expound on by using the example of nature and its renewal process. In the volcanic process, deep within the earth's crust magma forms, pressure develops, an eruption happens, lava flows, and then new land is formed. Heat creates growth, either through expansion or a breakdown. If it happens through expansion, the capacity of the given area is stretched. If it happens through a breakdown, an existing form melts to make a new form. So applying this to life, when tough times happen they leave you feeling not the best, get you heated up, and you feel like things are falling apart. However, know that this disintegrative process could be breaking down an existing structure (a figurative one) that is blocking or masking a realization or a renaissance within. The hard part is to feel it, go with it, experience every aspect of the situation, and trust the outcome. This will probably not be comfortable, but as you know, with a certain amount of pain comes growth. You have done it before and chances are you will experience this a few more times in your life, but hopefully you will do so with the awareness and knowledge that the growth process will prove beneficial in the long run and all will be OK! Just as things break down in our lives due to an emergency and we are able to grow and lead meaningful lives going forward, I can draw on that in future situations that reflect difficulty and upheaval. I know that all will be OK; no matter what happens there will be a benefit to it. This breakdown will essentially reveal the true essence or brilliance of a situation from its core level. Much like the volcanic process, its breakdown creates incredibly fertile earth . . . a renewal. As applied to life, the stripping process most likely will provide a new perspective on how you can view things, a new way to live, and a stretching of your capacity for that much more!

As I often say, "Can't take the heat? Stay in the kitchen!"

Questions to Ponder:

Would you allow yourself to feel the full spectrum of an uncomfortable life situation in order to gain incredible growth and awareness?

_____

_____

_____

_____

Have you existed outside of your zone of comfort emotionally, physically, or mentally for a sustained amount of time? If so, how and for what duration?

_____

_____

_____

_____

If not, how can you see yourself doing so, and in what capacity (emotionally, physically, or mentally)?

_____

_____

_____

_____

Can you recall a time when you came through a difficult situation and gained a gift from the eventual outcome? Write about your experience.

_____

_____

_____

_____

By reflecting on past experiences that were out of your comfort zone, how you existed in that situation, and how you were feeling emotionally, you have an opportunity to view the situation from another perspective. This reflection is happening now, so you are able to see it free of the heaviest of emotions that you felt during that time and can make concise observations about what your behavior was. This will reveal your ability to navigate through the discomfort during that time, and it will also tell you what you are now able to handle emotionally, physically, and mentally.

Recognizing the gift from the eventual outcome indicates your allowance—the allowance to see your way through to the end and feel all of the sensations that went along with it, despite the potential fear of things not ending up well. So again, by reflecting on this past experience and outcome you can see where you are now and how this has changed your life for the better. Sometimes people reflect on their childhood or previous years and say, "There were tough times, but I don't regret a thing because it brought me to where I am right now." Having this awareness and gratitude will ultimately add in a positive way to your life.

Conditional Happiness

"The ultimate is to become Desire-Less." —Yogi E

Have you ever said, "I'll be happy when I feel better, get in shape, go on vacation, get a promotion," etc.? Those things might be the key to happiness, but let's think about that for a moment. Are you possibly basing your happiness on results, outcomes, or situations outside of yourself? If so, that is putting a lot of responsibility and dependence on something in the future that hasn't even occurred (and there are no guarantees that it will). So then what? Does that mean you remain in abeyance, waiting for that ideal moment to come, and when and if that happens, then you can be happy, fulfilled, and satisfied? It seems silly to waste so much time on something that doesn't exist. This is time that can be spent feeling happy, joyous, and satisfied.

When your thoughts are somewhere in the future, it takes you out of the NOW, and one of the products is that you can potentially miss out on opportunities and golden moments that are in your immediate grasp. If you develop an awareness to dial in to the present, that's where your thoughts will be; they won't be scattered and propelled into the future, stealing away the fruit of your present moment or the contentedness of your spirit. Try it. I'm sure there is something in the moment that can put a smile on your face. Engaging someone or something with all of your attention brings a quality and fulfillment to that moment. Get all the way in the water, feel, experience, and live!

Basing your happiness on conditions is a surefire way to remain un-still and unsettled, because you are perpetually in the want mode. Being in a constant desire mode fragments your thoughts and places a great onus on expectation. Having unfulfilled expectations can lead to disappointment and sadness. If you have enough of those expectations out there, when they don't give the return that you want, well, you fill in the blank! On the flip side, let's say that you gain this moment of happiness because you achieve the result that you desired. Yippy yahoo. Now what? Do you become unhappy again once the polish and newness wear off? Or do you say, "I'm satisfied; game over"? It seems as if this could be a constant cycle of desiring, achieving, achieving, desiring—the proverbial cat chasing its tail. Give it a thought and see if this applies to an aspect of your life.

I will use the iPhone as an example of this. Steve Jobs came up with a product that was a game changer in the cellular and tech industry, and for the entire world as well. Everyone wanted an iPhone. It wasn't a rarity to wait in lines days long (literally) to obtain one, and still isn't! However, technology changes at a fast pace, and that equates to upgrades, changes, and new phones. This means what was once the shiny new must-have is no longer, and the latest and greatest must be obtained. This cycle has trained consumers to look for the upgraded models as soon as they purchase the new one and have it in their hands. The polish of the new fades soon after the Apple announcement bell rings, and what was once all the rage is quickly forgotten. This is the cat chasing its tail, in a constant cycle of desiring, achieving, achieving, and desiring.

Have goals, yes, but shift your thoughts to the present moment if they are out there in future land. Find joy and happiness right here and now. Have appreciation for where you are and what is going on in the present. Live as contentedly as you can, with what you have and where you are right now. Have peace in knowing that you have goals and desires that you are working toward, and once that happens, wonderful—but enjoy the journey it took to get there as well as the destination.

Questions to Ponder:

Life is a series of moments. How do you want yours to be lived?

_____

_____

_____

_____

Are you conditional with your happiness at times? If so, is your happiness dependent on something else?

_____

_____

_____

_____

Have you ever tried to enjoy the journey without focusing on the end result?

Take hold and capture your thoughts on paper about your moments and how you want to spend them, and recognize conditional aspects of your life to allow expression of the answers within. Through this, you will be able to identify the conditions you've currently put in place and sort them out individually as they pertain to your happiness. You may find that by weeding these things out and seeing them for what they are, you will not need them to be a barometer for your happiness. Let's say from these writings you find that you are basing your happiness on a day of the week like Friday, because Friday is the end of the workweek for you and this means you are free to do whatever out of the confines of fill in the blank. In other words, you're not happy until Friday comes. This is now something that you recognize and have put down on paper, and you begin to think that you can be happy every day of the week, not just Friday. You no longer use the day of the week as a barometer for you happiness. This makes it that much easier to delve into your present moment and live it fully without a condition dictating your next move.

Brooklyn

Brooklyn! There's no other place like it in the world; it's rich in culture, history, and diversity. So many facets meld into this one borough of New York. Each neighborhood has its own style and background, its own smells and tastes of cultural delicacies. A cornucopia of assorted cultures and lifestyles are woven into this fantastic slice of the world! The folks from Brooklyn are a unique bunch. You've got all types of nationalities and religions living, existing, and experiencing each other within 321 square miles and the more than 205,000 acres of this wonderful place!

I chose to write about Brooklyn because it is where I was born and raised. While there, I was exposed to many different types of people and the beat and essence of New York. I consider myself lucky to have been a part of that and to have had that experience in my life. This in turn gave me the ability to exist with an open heart and ready for the way things are today . . .

There are places (and I lived in one) that unfortunately don't have diversity, culture, or anything like that. Actually, they are quite plain and devoid of any expressive creativity, expansive thought process, and originality. You could even say that the inhabitants of these places live a master-planned, cattle, and cookie-cutter existence! Having experienced the other side of the spectrum by living in a diversely populated area and in another without diversity, I can see the extreme contrast that exists between the two. I think that one of the effects of not having diversity, culture, etc., and having plenty of existing sameness perpetuates intolerance.

This sameness can be in thought, outward appearances, and how one navigates through life. So if you don't look, act, or think like those who are within that context, you are prejudged for not conforming to their uniform.

Body art and tattoos are good examples of this. A person who has a full sleeve of tattoos or piercings may be asked to cover up their arms or take their jewelry off in the workplace because it's not considered professional or it could possibly offend clients or patrons. By forcing people to do this, society is saying that they are not presenting themselves in the same context as a person with a professional appearance, and this may turn away potential business. Along the same lines, people with tattoos and piercings are not viewed highly by the general public, because body art has a negative stigma attached to it. Another example of this is facial hair (beards); in certain arenas, it is not an acceptable look. Both examples reflect pre-judging for nonconforming attributes against the uniform of a group. This judgment can breed fear, because those who are judging don't know or can't identify, so it may be threatening. When one is presented the same life scenario over and over without diversity, the capacity to accept, understand, and tolerate is limited or nonexistent because the experience is limited. If you only exist within the box, how would you know what goes on beyond it?

I think our world in its current state is in need of a lot of love, acceptance, tolerance, and understanding. Far too often we hear about wars, racism, hatred, intolerance, and on and on. If one is willing to start within one's heart and mind, then that love and acceptance can reach our kids, the streets, neighborhoods, cities, states, and (hopefully) eventually the world!

"Diversity may be the hardest thing for a society to live with, and perhaps the most dangerous thing for a society to be without." —William Sloane Coffin, Jr.

Scientists have become increasingly aware that biological diversity is the key to the survival of all species (plants, animals, all living things). I believe that cultural diversity is likewise a key to the survival of humankind. If we all think, act, look, and believe the same way, we won't survive because we can't adapt to the dynamic and changing conditions of this planet. Even dog breeders can tell you that pure breeds have a higher incidence of disease than mixed breed dogs do. Diversity is good, healthy, and necessary!

<u>Questions to Ponder:</u>

Are you a box dweller?

_____

_____

_____

_____

Where do your limitations lie with regard to being tolerant of others, if you have any?

_____

_____

_____

_____

By identifying an aspect of yourself that lacks tolerance and acceptance, you can begin to look at why you feel that way and how you came to conceptualize those aspects. This is a tough one, because it's difficult to see yourself critically. I say critically, because you're being asked to view your intolerance and potential prejudices in order to uncover an inherent limitation. Even if you don't see this as a limitation, there's got to be a reason why you're reading this book, right?

Looking into the limitations of how you accept others is an exercise of honesty and exploration. Unmasking what lies beneath a judgment brings you the opportunity to find a reason for validating yourself through the assessment of another. Being honest and exposing your judgments will hopefully be enough to shift your mind to promote another way of perceiving.

Our Wake-Up Call

The events of April 24, 2008, will forever shape my life. You never think it can happen to you! Well, it happened to me, and I am a changed person because of it. You often hear about unfortunate situations that happen to people and how those people miraculously find resolve, peace, and a renewed sense of living. That is often followed by an incredible amount of humility and gratitude. I am living and feeling all of the above. When you think life is going to end, that's when you wake up! A single point of focus occurs and nothing else is on the radar. It is a complete immersion in the will to sustain life. Almost losing someone you love can bring you face to face with your darkest fears. It brings you to your raw and exposed core.

After completing a run with my husband, Keith, we returned home and the strangest thing happened. He became distracted and was acting oddly, moving his arms and looking around. I thought he was kidding, but then he fell to the ground without bending his knees, just like a tree falling down. I screamed and noticed there was blood coming from his mouth. I shouted to my daughter to call 911. It was as if everything was in slow motion. I noticed he was still breathing but not conscious; his body was stiff but convulsing. I knew he was getting oxygen, but I didn't know what was happening. Turns out he was having a seizure. It seemed like it took forever for the paramedics to arrive. On the ride to the hospital (I chose to ride up front because I couldn't handle being in the back with him), the ambulance driver calmed me as much as he could. He was stern and factual and said, "Your husband is going to the best hospital facility for his situation; he's going to be in good hands." I held tightly to those words to comfort me, for I had nothing else to grab on to. In the ER, they diagnosed and treated Keith after many hours and many more seizures. While that was going on, I sat alone in the waiting area feeling incredibly scared and holding on to whatever hope I could grasp. I was way beyond my edge. The seizure had been caused by a tumor in the right parietal lobe of Keith's brain. A few months later, he had surgery to remove the tumor. The surgery was a success, and we were immeasurably grateful for that outcome.

This really put into focus what matters to us, and how we choose to spend our precious time. Although the situation that happened was unfortunate, we NOW see it as a gift. While it was occurring and afterward, we couldn't possibly comprehend this concept. It was still too new and raw to us. The gift is seeing and feeling the importance of our moments and what our focus is. Our journey is filled with love, passion, awareness, appreciation, and inspiration—it is not destination oriented. I never want it to end. It's what Keith fought so hard to come back to, it's what I prayed so hard that we could continue, it's what we live for every day, the journey of life and the experience of living! Living from the heart is the result for us. Not taking each other or life for granted, for we know how precious it is. We've relocated and are quite happy with our surroundings. The incident prompted us to be in the location where we wanted to be, and live the way we wanted to live, free of the obligatory actions from our former life. Now our lives are filled with enjoying our home, which we remodeled exactly to our preferences, and loving our adopted rescue cats Skibby and Barrington, who fill our lives with so much unconditional love! We take frequent mini and mega vacations, go to lots of movies, and, best of all, Keith, my daughter Tiana, and I relax together in the evenings. It's not that we didn't relax together before Keith's situation, it's just that now we cherish it that much more!

I share this with you because this experience moved us so powerfully in so many ways. I would like you to take from this experience the importance of being true to your life and what is important to you. Live from your heart and live authentically.

Keith had another surgery in January 2014 to remove a tumor that grew back in the same spot. He is healthy, and we remain true to living from our heart and experiencing our lives fully. One thing that became evident to me was that life was fragile. Seeing and experiencing that fragility firsthand was a lightbulb moment for me. I am forever left with an appreciation for the life that sustains my family and me. With that knowledge in my heart, I recognize, cultivate, and nurture my connections to my family, friends, other living things, and my surroundings on a much more conscious level. I engage on a deeper level when I communicate with others, and that validates for me the connection to life we all share, as well as the fragility we all share as well. This fills my heart with compassion every day.

Questions to Ponder:

Do you feel you may be taking life for granted? If so, how? If no, state why.

_____

_____

_____

_____

Are you living or existing the way you'd like to? If not, how can you start implementing ways to do so? Living day to day in a routine can lend itself to being staid in action, thought, and expanse. It's not that you are taking life for granted on purpose, it just that it isn't always on your radar. This exercise asks you to move this awareness onto your radar by directly stating what it is that you do take for granted. You can start with a category such as your friends and loved ones. How are you missing the opportunity to recognize your connection to them? What do you appreciate about them, and will you let them know that? These are a couple of examples of how to dial in to what you may be dialed out of. Continue to write down these things, and you will open your heart and mind to new possibilities and aspects of your receptiveness and appreciation.

Stating how you want to live is the threshold for making that manifest. You may find by doing so, you arrive at feelings that you hadn't thought of, or unearth a few feelings that have been buried. If this happens, it is a plus, because that could inspire new ways of existing. It's another addition to your list of criteria. These inspirations and new feelings should also be written down so you have them displayed and available to work with as you move toward a new way of living. The next thing to look at is how you can begin to make this list come alive by implementing changes that you can attain almost immediately. Let's say one thing on your list is to change your living environment to a more conducive space that feels good to you. Look at the objects in your home on walls or shelves, and see if you really like them. If not, begin to remove the objects from your space and replace them with something that resonates with you. Another thing that you can do immediately is to get rid of clutter in a room (or all rooms) and see what the free space does for your creativity level.

Starting the process is the most important thing. Do it with the awareness that it is a process, and it all cannot be done at once. Change what you can at first, then set intentions and goals to reach the rest of your list. It will come in time, but while it's in progress you will feel good about it along the way, because you're getting things done according to your true needs.

Addressing It Right Then and There

Bothered, disturbed, confused?

I'm sure many of you have encountered a situation or interaction that has left you feeling pretty unsettled, confused, or worried. Have you ever had a conversation with someone and it seems to be going fine, and then it takes a strange turn? As this change is happening, you try to make sense out of it, but there's just no figuring it out or getting back to the easygoing interaction from moments ago. The meeting concludes, and you are left asking yourself, "Did I say something wrong? What happened?" This can be quite unsettling and can linger in your mind for the rest of the day or even longer. What would make it better is obtaining a direct answer.

Unfortunately, most times the reason for the skewed interaction doesn't present itself, and that unsettled feeling gets pushed down somewhere. We basically exist with all of this suppressed junk inside of us for a very long time. This "somewhere" is also filled with guilt, fear, and other experiences we choose not to face along the way. It's easy to see how these feelings get layered, mixed together, and as a result you don't feel the best. Subsequently, you may overreact to a situation or get angry and not even know why or where this behavior originated. How could you identify the origin when these feelings are all mushed together?

If we could learn how to deal with difficult issues and interactions as they occur, we might be able to avoid prolonged feelings of irritation, disruption, anger, or any other negative feelings that might arise. Using the previous example (when the negative turn happened during the conversation), addressing it with the person right then and there would have provided the opportunity to find out what happened and possibly get an answer to the troublesome situation. Hopefully the person would respond and all would be known, dealt with, and done! But what happens when you are unable to communicate or there is no other person involved? Then it has to be dealt with and reconciled in your own mind, and that's the tricky part.

"Rule your mind, or it will rule you." —Horace Mann

By nature we are creatures of comfort; we seek to have it in most areas of life. So, having a Q&A session with the person to find out what went wrong is motivated in part by the need to have comfort and peace within. The hard part is facing and confronting the "dis-ease" within the mind. It's not a comfortable thing to do. You must ask questions about why something is bothering you, get to the root cause of the problem, find out why it is affecting you (to whatever degree) and what it is that you are not allowing yourself to see or experience. The answers to these questions may not be easy to obtain, but believe me, they are there. You hold the key. Once they are brought to light and confronted, you then can deal with each issue one at a time, instead of having them all intermingled in a confused state, which causes some of the prolonged unhappiness and dissatisfaction in life. If you undertake this intrinsic process, it will likely provide insight, answers, and much-needed healing over time. Be fearless!

Questions to Ponder:

Would you have a difficult time questioning someone directly after a confusing or not so great interaction? If yes, why? If no, why?

_____

_____

_____

_____

Do you think you have a lot of suppressed emotions? If so, can you sort them into categories such as guilt, anger, fear, etc.? Now describe the emotion attached to the category. For example, create a table with categories along the top that represent your emotions—anger, guilt, fear, etc. Below each emotion, fill in a word or two that describes the emotion. You can create this chart in your notebook or journal, or you can use the template provided below. Here's what it will look like:

Anger	Guilt	Fear	Joy
Someone disrespecting you	Hurting someone you love	Not knowing an outcome	Feeling happy

This separates your feelings out, and it's quite powerful because your feelings are being conveyed and categorized! This exercise allows you to look at yourself from a clear perspective, and when this happens, you can proceed to heal the actual areas within yourself that need to be healed. This sorting and healing will aid how you perceive situations, how you respond to them, and it will ultimately build your ability to process emotions efficiently. When you're at a point of processing efficiently, then you are confident in knowing who you are and how you're resonating. This leads to not needing to question why someone is acting a certain way, because the once-open insecure space has been addressed by writing and sorting out the emotions, thereby filling that open space. Outside forces will always be; how you respond to those forces is up to you. You control that!

On the following table, fill in the four categories on top with your emotions (see the preceding template example). Then, under each category, list the corresponding emotions.

Oh, the Drama

Sadly, it seems to be a growing human trait to rely on external forces to fulfill a need, provide happiness, excuses, and satisfaction. This is running wild throughout our society as a collective. Seeking something from outside yourself will *often* result in failure. Relying on an object, person, or situation to bring you happiness may not fill you entirely. The reason is the desired effect is temporary. When you place responsibility for your existence on an external force, you have also put a condition on your true satisfaction. In essence, you are saying that you will be happy on the condition that this outside source comes through. The place to look and extract authentic happiness is within yourself, not from anything external.

"Happiness is not something ready made. It comes from your own actions." Dalai Lama XIV

People also use external forces to create, by way or drama, a state of turmoil, sadness, and repetitive, senseless actions. Drama diverts from what is real and true, or keeps the self from reaching its highest and true potential. The mind, on some conscious or unconscious level, thinks that suppression is safe, contained, and therefore there is no need to go any further to expand the thought process to change the situation for the better. It's too much work. Pseudo-contentment can be found in mediocrity and rudimentary existence. The need to keep the drama and sadness going is in high demand because that's the tool individuals use to remain in turmoil. The ego thrives off this endless loop of codependent behavior. It is such a strong, useful pattern providing the exact platform to keep people in this victimized, suppressed, "woe is me," needy, and unhappy existence. Now some may say, "What, are you kidding me, who would want to live that way?" I say to that, do your homework and see how many people complain about the same things over and over. Do an experiment and see for yourself. Don't believe anything I say, go and experience it for yourself. Not all folks are this way, but the majority of our society opts for this type of behavior. You can witness it in people who often complain about their weight and are very upset about it, but do nothing about it from meal to meal. They just remain in complaint mode and don't move from there. It's easier for them to remain where they are instead of doing what it takes to get out of it.

You've heard of *self-fulfilling prophecies* or *black clouds*. These are the types of clichés or labels people also use to become or remain suppressed. Let's not forget to add tumultuous relationships to the mix! Those are BIG contributors to the enabling thing I'm talking about. *Remaining with people who keep the codependent flame of dysfunction burning bright and strong* is a common way to rely on an external force to remain in a state of suppression. Without recognition as to what is happening in your life as it pertains to habitual states of discord, it could potentially suppresses any chance to shift out of that state. Be proactive in your own life by defining parameters and limitations around issues of discord. Doing so will enable you to manage what is in front of you step by step. You are now acknowledging and *managing* your situation. This will override the suppressed nature and bring personal empowerment into your life.

Here's an example of setting parameters and limitations for relationships. Let's say there's a person who needs to people-please in order to feel good about himself. He may set himself up with a group or individuals who will be receptive to him and who will give him the thing that he needs. Let's also say that these individuals don't have the best of moral standards and often make poor societal and life decisions. After being involved in this connection for some time, it's evident that there are some dysfunction and dependency issues that surround this association. The person recognizes this state of discord and makes a choice to make a change. He takes action by (1) acknowledging his need to people-please, (2) seeing what relationships he cultivated in order to perpetuate his need to people-please, (3) reviewing what negative associations or outcomes he created in his life by being associated with this group, (4) eliminating and limiting the relationships that create dysfunction and dependency one by one. By taking these actions, self-empowerment is born, and this person takes hold of managing his life! Recognizing and seeing firsthand his own value, by doing for *himself*, and appreciating his own ability and strength contributed to his ability to eliminate the need to people-please! He found his own power and filled the space *need* once filled.

Many people settle for being a victim of circumstance or involve themselves in limiting situations that contribute to their means of suppression. Being a proactive participant in your own journey by adopting new perspectives and taking action is the key to propel you into a happy, balanced, and satisfied state of existing.

Questions to Ponder:

Do you see a pattern of drama and a reliance on external forces within your own life?

_____

_____

_____

_____

If so, how can you shift or change those patterns? Make a list.

_____

_____

_____

_____

Can you take any ideas from the example given above to help you answer this question? Although your situation may not look like the example, it can give you an idea of how to go about the process.

Guilt

I'm sure you have fallen victim to guilt, felt it, or even used it as a tool sometime in your life. It certainly produces strong feelings that might inhibit or provoke you to action or inaction.

When you feel guilty about something, it can dwell in your heart and psyche for a while, even to the extent that all of your actions from that point forward are dictated by that guilt. As adults, it's hard enough to exist with our own idiosyncrasies, let alone add feelings of guilt on top of that, so when it comes to the little ones, we must be aware of their fragility and sponge-like ability to take everything in.

Often children are introduced to guilt when a parent makes them feel shame about a choice or action they took. As an example, when parents are not pleased with the grades their children are receiving at school, they confront their kids with words like "Your friend Joe has good grades. Why aren't you like Joe with your studies? It makes me so sad and angry that you have grades like this." This makes their children feel shame and guilt because they feel that they are responsible for their parents' anger and sadness. They also feel that if they had better grades, their parents would feel better and they would be looked upon favorably, just as Joe is by his parents.

Guilt can make an impression on how these children view themselves. In essence, they are given the message that they aren't enough and don't measure up to their parents' happiness. This impression can follow kids whenever they are being tested in life and in school. The aftereffect is they will perform to please rather than to succeed for themselves. Instead of communicating about the situation, guilt is used to make a lasting burn in a child's mind that can potentially affect the decisions he or she makes going forward in life. It's something like getting burned once and not wanting to feel that pain ever again, so by virtue of this, those actions won't be repeated. The child is now equipped with the experience of how guilt works, the effective emotional impact it makes, and how it is a means of manipulation to control others' behavior.

Manipulation is a false means of power used under the guise of fear. This means of control is effective and quick. That's why others will catch on and begin to use guilt as a tool for themselves. It's deceitful and hurtful, and I'm sure we all have experienced this at one time or another. It's important to recognize when we use guilt and when it's being used against us so we can stop guilt from embedding itself and creating more of a disconnect.

Guilt may also inhibit your natural flow and freedom when it comes to decision-making, progression, and growth. It keeps you tied to a situation or a circumstance because you would feel guilty if you changed it or made another choice. You don't want to disappoint, so you remain bound, suppressing your existence because you are dragging around an old scar. It probably would take a lot for someone to turn his or her back and break those chains, but the discomfort felt by the short-term action of disconnecting from the old may prevent a lifetime of enduring the pain of suppression.

Think about the allowance factor. Are you allowing shame in the door to exist invasively, sacrificing your free will? If you follow or do something for a while, it becomes routine and a natural part of your life. Essentially, by this allowance you go about life giving your power away. The outside force or person that placed this feeling of guilt or shame into your life was allowed in and made itself commonplace. To recognize the intrusion and become aware of what has been done lets you to begin the banishing process, meaning that the influence will lose its power over you. You are now empowered and freed from the chains of guilt.

On the flip side, if you put guilt on the back burner as a tool and wait to use it when you deem that's necessary, think twice before implementing. NOT doing so breaks the cycle. It starts with you. You have the ability to enforce change in your life, and the example that you provide could possibly be infectious, thereby having a positive impact on many other lives. AWARENESS is the key.

<u>Questions to Ponder:</u>

Has guilt found its way into your life? If so, please describe it.

_____

_____

_____

_____

Or are you using it for one reason or another? If so, then why? Please describe.

_____

_____

_____

_____

If so, consider releasing it. If you think about it, does it really hold any value?

Hamster Wheel

Have you ever seen a hamster in a Habitrail or running on a wheel and felt bad for him because his space is limited? No matter how elaborate the connection tube systems are, the hamster still covers the same ground every day.

Does this resemble anything in your life? Are you on a hamster wheel, going around and around, covering the same ground mentally, physically, or geographically? Have you ever considered seeing life through different eyes, trying things that you have never experienced? I'm sure that some of you live experientially and are willing to try different things, but many people don't go out of their normal sphere of experience. We are creatures of comfort and often seek to find that place, so thinking out of the box or off the wheel may take you out of your level of comfort in some form or another. Just by virtue of doing something differently you can potentially walk the road less traveled. Even within the course of a normal day, you can create anew just by shifting a thought process or doing something like ordering a different beverage at the coffee shop! The possibilities are endless for how you can change things up.

I know when things become rote and repetitive I get uninspired, so in order for me to break out of that space, I have to put a spin or two into the mix and see what happens. For me, that means doing things differently on the weekend. We usually do our weekly grocery shopping on a Sunday, so instead we go shopping Saturday night and that frees up the next day to do whatever we desire. On that Sunday, we do absolutely nothing! We stay home, watch movies, and have ample provisions from our trip to the market the night before. It's perfect. We all are relaxed and enjoy the spontaneity of our day together; it takes us out of a routinized weekend schedule and provides a refreshing reset for our minds. This off-the-wheel moment provides the room we needed to experience something different, even if it is for one day.

Here are some examples of how to introduce change or step off the wheel:

Mental

Having unique conversations rather than the same old hamster wheel speak may just turn on that lightbulb of genius that we all have inside.

Geographical

If you travel to the same place every year, perhaps next year you should consider a new destination. Travel can enhance our lives tremendously because you experience yourself in another backdrop. This is especially true when you travel to places you have never been, or out of the country. By seeing and experiencing cultures other than your own, you expand your sphere of tolerance and capacity.

Physical

See if there is anything you would like to change or enhance with regard to your body, and if so, then go for it! Perhaps create an exercise regimen and a refreshing change to your diet to create physical change in your body. Or, you may feel that your body needs a stretching regimen to give you better posture and more energy. Maybe you want a different hair color or style that will change your look for the season. Whatever change or enhancement means for you, take steps to make it happen. Within your home or workplace, if there are any changes or shifts you could make to create a different experience, go for it! If you want to move your furniture or purchase a new piece to transform the look of a room in your home, that is a fast way to obtain a result. Try adding items of personal significance to your office space. Small desk plants and colorful accent pieces such as picture frames, artwork, or lamps can also provide enhancement to your space at work. If it's possible, purchase your own desk chair that is ergonomically perfect for you to provide the comfort that you need throughout the day. By implementing these little things, your overall feeling in the space at home and work will be transformed, and that will hopefully inspire new ways to enhance your life.

It doesn't matter what your situation is, you can always find ways to get off the wheel.

Questions to Ponder:

Do you feel that you live aspects of your life on the hamster wheel?

_____

_____

_____

_____

What are some quick changes you can make in those areas to implement change?

_____

_____

_____

_____

If you haven't noticed yet, the common thread through these ponderings is awareness. Becoming aware of what is occurring in your life is key to making the changes that are necessary to whatever it is that needs to change. Awareness is the first and most powerful portion of your journey of change, because you have allowed yourself to actually see what is occurring. With this acknowledgment, you have the power to transform your life.

That being said, by answering the questions above you will be able to identify areas where things are being repeated and create ideas to break the present repetitive conditions.

Staying on the Horizon Line

You're standing on a beautiful beach looking out toward the water and your eyes focus on the horizon, a long, even, and consistent line that stretches farther than the eye can see.

There is something to be said about this steady state. There is a flow, a rhythm, and a consistency that being in this state brings. Peace and ease are sure to follow. How important is it for you to live your life in a steady state? Have you even thought about it? Do you even want it? If this is something that sounds desirous, then it's time to reflect upon your emotional state and its fluctuations.

Having consistent emotions can provide a flow and an easeful state, as well as confidence. Let's say you have two co-workers you interact with daily. You observe that Person A is basically easy to communicate with, and her greetings and responses are genuine, short, and effective. Person B is also easy to communicate with, but you find that the type of greeting and response he gives are in direct relation to how he is feeling that day or that moment. Person A maintains a consistency irrespective of what's on her plate. Person B is all over the board, letting his emotions dictate his actions. Going forward you would probably feel more confident with person A's ability to perform at a consistent level, and would much rather work alongside that person when working on a project deadline. Reason being, the probability of her productivity would be higher than the person who is emotionally tethered and therefore may not be able to perform to his highest ability.

When your emotions dictate your responses to the degree that those you are interacting with are unable to gain a true sense of what you are communicating, it's hard for people to trust what you're conveying. The information they receive is filtered through or clouded by emotion, and this prevents an authentic response from shining through. The consistency the moment requires isn't being reflected. I would certainly prefer that the pilot of a plane I'm on or the surgeon performing my operation be in a steady state. Consistency brings assurance, clarity, and the ability to execute at a pure level without a filter or distortion—hence the appeal of the steady-state Person A, and a horizon line.

Every day is different, and our reactions to things, other people, and situations are always changing. Mental flexibility is a key component to achieving consistency in your daily life. When we make or hear statements such as "It wasn't like it was yesterday" or "It used to be this way, but now it's changed," we are making comparisons. If you compare one situation to another, find that they are different, and you're not *OK* or satisfied with that fact, you will feel that you are missing out or that you should be getting a better outcome from a situation. When this happens, you have a choice: stay dissatisfied or move on and change how you think about the situation. If the choice is to change your perception, you must gain mental flexibility. This can happen through acceptance, seeing things as they are and keeping judgment and comparison out of the equation, being flexible enough to allow another thought process to take place, or just meeting things where they are. *This will bring consistency of peace and ease* during the ever-changing dynamics of daily life and interactions.

I, for one, have reflected back on many occasions to when I was younger and how I looked back then, even seeing older photos of myself and saying, "Wow, look how young I was." Then the journey of the mind takes me to how I would like to look or to feel again, or I compare my abilities back then to now and want to have those abilities back in some respect. Then I start to feel bad because I know that is not obtainable and I can't be that person again. This is a true mind game—that I should be something else—and it keeps me from who and what I am presently. This is when I have to implement mental flexibility in order to meet myself where I am and remove comparison. It brings the consistency and peace I need to change this behavior.

I've shown how being in a steady state enhances the integrity of an interaction. Now I will give an example of staying on that horizon line as it applies to thoughts and preferences.

The range between feeling high and low is large. The emotional opposition can make you feel unbalanced, sad, or disappointed. Let's take a look at a situation to show this range.

The date for your long-awaited vacation to the tropics is a few weeks away! During this time, your excitement and feelings about this trip are building every day, and you feel great. Now let's fast-forward to your arrival back home. The feelings are NOT going to be as high and "feel good" as they were prior to and during the vacation. This is due in part to societal conditioning when we categorize days as TGIF, Wednesday hump day, casual Fridays, and of course that Mondays are just flat-out no good. It doesn't have to be this way. Having the ability to wrap your mind around returning from a vacation, going to work on Mondays, or anything else that may produce a less-than-stellar feeling can provide a peaceful satisfaction or state. Yes, vacations are exciting, Fridays are awesome, and Mondays, not so much! Vacation is not an everyday occurrence, and therefore it's awesome and may be better than everyday life. Many may concur with this, but there is another way to construct it in your mind. We have control over the associations we make to an event, a day of the week, or an occurrence. If you have a positive and happy association with vacationing and Fridays and whatever else, that is great! But having control over associations ensures that one event or thing doesn't get more "happys" than another as a function of your perception. If you perceive that your happiness is conditioned by a future event or thing, you prevent potential happiness from filling your life in the present moment. Meet a trip or a Friday with joy, but meet Mondays or having no trip with joy too. What prevents you from achieving this is mental fluctuations and judgment. If the mind is going to these extreme conditional contrasts, it is not still and steady.

Recognizing when there is potential for these mental fluctuations can greatly enhance your ability to remain consistent throughout your day. *Balance is a neutral space that feels organic and free of effort!* That is the key to staying on the horizon line. Balance! This balance can be achieved by *Being Happy Now!* Understand that being happy now or at some other time is a choice, and this choice is usually conditional (in the above examples, vacations or Fridays). Being happy now is not out there somewhere in the cosmos, it's inside of you now. All that needs to happen is for you to make the choice to be happy with what is going on presently. I'm not saying to be happy about misfortune or a bad event. I am saying to be happy within yourself, feel the joy that you can create and have in every moment. Keep the context of happiness, what that means to you, and ride that feeling all day, every day! Wake up on Monday and say to yourself, "I will be happy today, I will think good things, and I will be aware of my choice to be happy moment by moment." When that vacation or weekend ends, your ability to remain balanced on the horizon line will be evident because you won't have had much fluctuation of the mind.

"Happiness is not a matter of intensity but of balance, order, rhythm and harmony" —Thomas Merton

Questions to Ponder:

Can you list ways in which you may be out of balance in your thoughts, preferences, and interactions?

_____

_____

_____

_____

What is the first thing you can easily implement to achieve a steady state in interactions and emotions?

_____

_____

_____

_____

Identifying areas of imbalance will lead you right to your creative ability to produce change in those areas and find steady state awareness. Also using *happiness* now as a means to this change could also influence how to go about this change.

The Energy of Your Relationships

How many relationships do you still have from twenty or thirty years ago? I'll bet that there are few, if any. That's because energy shifts, life changes, circumstances change, and people lose touch. It's natural. When this happens in a natural way, the relationship dissolves and slides off your radar in a neat and clean fashion. What you do have are the memories and experiences (negative or positive) from the relationship that added to your life and helped you become the person you are right now. That is the gift of connection.

Sometimes you outgrow a relationship and may no longer hold "like energy" with that person. Once in a while you should evaluate whether the relationships you are in still serve you and in what capacity they impact your life. Our lives span many years, and most of those years are spent interacting with many people. We form lifelong bonds with some, others we casually cross paths with, and with some we have cohesive relationships, but as time goes on, the common place you once shared may no longer exist. In this case, there will probably be a reluctance to evaluate and release or terminate the relationship because of habit, familiarity, or fear of the unknown. That lack of action can possibly create an irritant or a constant reminder that the connection, which was once very much cohesive, is now going in two separate directions. Each person goes about life in their own fashion, but when their paths meet, it is no longer on smooth common ground—possibly because of the awkwardness of the dissolved relationship and the lack of action taken to address it. Some will end the relationship immediately, while others may take no action or initiative to move on, so they continue to bump into each other energetically along their separate paths while remaining connected to their relationship with each other. These energetic bumps can have a great impact on everyday life and how you view and interact with the world. If you have enough of them, they can pile up and turn up the intensity. Compare this to being miserable in your job. This misery or dissatisfaction carries over to your nonworking life because you go to work every day, and it is a large part of your daily existence. It piles up, and misery becomes a big part of your life.

You often hear of married couples who stay together for the *sake of the kids*. So they stay together despite the frequent arguments, lack of communication, sleeping in separate rooms, and perhaps infidelity. Their attempts to save the marriage have been exhausted, and the relationship is functioning on empty, devoid of the love, care, and attention that cultivates a marriage. Do you think that the kids won't feel the negative underlying energy in the home every day? What example is being set for these children? Are they learning to sacrifice their own peace and happiness because they see their parents doing that? Are they learning that healthy, loving relationships are not important, nor is existing peacefully? Now, there may be some marriages that are over but the couple can stay together in a peaceful way for the sake of the kids or just for the familiar nature of it, because they've known it for a long time and they are friends. The key here is *in a peaceful way,* because if the situation doesn't bother either party and is not affecting the kids in a negative fashion, it could potentially remain that way forever or until the kids are grown or either person decides that enough is enough and takes action to leave the marriage. If this is the route taken, then it must be done in a loving way, with respect for each other and the many years they've spent together, and yes, for the children. By no means am I encouraging divorce, but I am encouraging heart happiness along with peace and ease.

"Yesterday is not ours to recover, but tomorrow is ours to win or lose." —Lyndon B. Johnson

The value of your peace and happiness should always be on the front burner, and you should not lose sight of the goal and purpose to be happy in life. It is easy for things to take a backseat and fall through the cracks, but your peace of heart and mind should not be taken for granted.

Perhaps this message will prompt you to evaluate the acquaintances, friendships, and relationships in your life. If no evaluation is necessary and you are perfectly content and happy with all of your connections, then Mazel tov! Good for you; that's exactly where you should be.

Questions to Ponder:

Do you have any relationships that are outdated and that should be addressed? If yes, would you consider doing so? List some ways that you would go about it.

_____

_____

_____

_____

If you wouldn't consider addressing these relationships, state the reasons why. Also, list how the relationship impacts you energetically when you interact with that person.

_____

_____

_____

_____

These questions are pointed and direct, and your answers should be the same. Be honest and clear about what you are feeling when writing your words. Honest answers indicate your true feelings about the relationships in question and will aid you in your process if you choose to address the situation. You will have it all worked out in your mind and heart prior to the communication. Therefore, no stone will be unturned and all will be there for your conveyance.

Grand Illusion

Some things are not as they seem! Especially when you don't experience them firsthand. In your mind, you picture things a certain way—that's all you can do because you're not directly involved with them. You may envision this other situation to be different or better compared to your present circumstances. This is purely a fantasy of the mind, taking you on a journey of its own liking. We've all heard the saying "The grass is greener on the other side of the fence." Well, that's easy to perceive, especially when you are not on the other side of the fence. Assuming that you will be better off *over the fence* is nothing but an assumption and may not be a fact. Needless to say, it's still an attractive notion that the other side is better. Of course it's attractive and enticing. Your mind is creating the perfect scenario according to your untouched and untapped desires! That's why I call it a grand illusion.

These thoughts don't occur circumstantially or realistically; all of this is playing out *upstairs* in the *Grand Dome Theater*. Let's say that you get to this supposed place, person, or circumstance. It won't be like anything in your prior visions or thoughts, because every situation is unique and unfolds in real time. In other words, it happens in the Now! Hey, there is nothing wrong with fantasy or envisioning things—that can be entertaining and a lot of fun, and it may even give you something to shoot for. But the authentic moment happens in real time and in the Now. Even if the unfolding process doesn't measure up to your expectations, that's OK because the experience may even be better—*that's right, better*—than you envisioned. The point is to remain flexible and open to what arises, free from immediate judgment that may hinder the organic experience. If a present circumstance or situation is creating "dis-ease" in your life and you find yourself thinking about how green the grass is on the other side, you first might want to evaluate how to create an easeful state with the present situation until it changes or resolves. Basically, the grass is greener where you water it! Nurture and appreciate what you have, and give yourself time to understand what it is that's creating the dis-ease. By doing this, you will clearly be able to identify what needs to change by creating an ease-filled state of being. The mind fluctuations will calm, and you will have the ability to see things from a neutral perspective. Try not to get wrapped up in the "What if?" or "How would it be?" Just keep the momentum building toward resolve. Often, you can get stuck in a place of non-movement because of the mind's strong hold on fear, the unknown, the need to settle, and satisfaction with an illusion. The drawback from this inaction may be one of regret and the proverbial "would've, should've, could've." Being proactive about your peace and happiness in life is paramount and should be treated as such. You are your most powerful advocate! Once you are ready to *experience* a new backdrop, do just that, experience it and decorate it to your heart's desire! No holds barred, live from your heart and make it the fantasy, the *all that and a bag of chips* dream experience that you've desired, then and only then will that be your true organic reality. It will be lived and loved in real time.

You should always be proactive about obtaining your peace and happiness.

"Make it so, Number One." —*Captain Jean-Luc Picard of the* Star Trek: The Next Generation

<u>Questions to Ponder:</u>

Are you holding yourself back from experiencing something new due to fear? If so, why? How can you change that?

_____

_____

_____

_____

Appreciation

Appreciation: we understand, need, give, and feel it. This is very powerful in so many ways because it is something very dear to the heart. When you have appreciation for something or someone, you know how that feels in your heart—it brings joy. So when appreciation is not given or received, it can make you feel rejected, used, or unworthy. Since you know what it feels like when *you have* appreciation, you feel emptiness when you are underappreciated or not appreciated at all. If you think about it, the reason you may feel that way is the expectation you have about that person's response to you. Or, the value you place on your own actions may not be equal to the value others who are witness to or in receipt of your actions place on them.

An example of this is at the workplace. You have been working above and beyond what your position requires in order for your department to succeed. Everyone knows the incredible effort that you put forth due to the imbalance of others doing their jobs inefficiently. Not only do your co-workers know this, the department manager is also well aware of it. Since the work is getting done and the department is meeting its numbers, the manager feels that there is no need to change how things are being done. You never get a raise in salary, nor are you recognized individually for your stellar efforts. This makes you feel unappreciated, as if the manager doesn't consider the value of your actions. He sees it as a functioning department, end of story. You're left feeling devalued, because you expect to have a positive return on all of your hard work. It's a judgment call.

Sometimes the result matches your expectation and other times it may fall very short. This reflects some of the issues with having expectations, since not everyone sees eye to eye. In the case of not being valued for your efforts, you could be proud of what you accomplished alone. It is an opportunity to see what you're capable of and the type of work ethic that you have to undertake such a task. Knowing your own self-worth and feeling satisfied with the outcome that you produced is enough to override the need to be recognized by another.

Even if you feel that you don't have expectations but you still feel underappreciated, it's due in part to your conditioning. From an early age, whenever you did something good, you got rewarded or commended. You were given attention and appreciation for your actions. Receiving this type of attention on a repeated basis made these conditional responses seem normal. As you went through life, you took with you the perception of the *normal* response of appreciation. You didn't see it as having an expectation. Instead, you viewed it as natural and normal.

Knowing the potential cause of feeling underappreciated can set you on a path of clarity and understanding. The moment you detach from these feelings of *lack* is the moment you will gain freedom. Knowing that you are enough by recognizing your *own* value and worth, irrespective of another's accolades or opinions, is the answer to feeling free of being less than or lacking. Keep the learned, cognized belief away from your *own* ability to meet the situation with self-actualization and balance. That will provide a real-time response to the moment. The issue of not being appreciated will no longer have power over your emotions because you will have released attachments of expectation. You'll be free just to be with what is. Just do things to do them, and don't worry about the response of others. You will gain much more satisfaction from the fact that YOU appreciate who you are and what you do. That holds a value for yourself that no one else can match! With that feeling of self-empowerment, you'll grow closer to confidence and joy in your life.

Find happiness within. This is a great way to start!

Questions to Ponder:

Do you value and appreciate who you are?

_____

_____

_____

_____

PART THREE

Another Perspective

This third and final part of the book ties all three parts together with an example and application type of reading. You will come across hints and references to what you've read previously, and you will see how they come together in the scenarios given. Part Three is comprised of seven sections, beginning with "The Mind – The Limited Edition" and ending with "Shedding the Layers." Each of these sections will give you another opportunity to associate your own situation to what you are reading, and hopefully each will encourage you to apply any inspiration you may receive to your own life. By reading these examples, you will directly see how roles influence patterns and behaviors. You will be able to identify the processes of the mind, ego, preferences, and behaviors as they pertain to each scenario.

The title of this part is "Another Perspective." It was written to give your mind another way to perceive the principles and examples from Parts One and Two. Seeing other ways these principles can infuse themselves into daily life can help you identify, associate, and assimilate the same process solutions in your own life.

The Mind – The Limited Edition

Life is like a game of pool. Envision a huge pool table that represents existence. On it there's a cue ball that represents you and there are the object balls that represent phenomena. When the cue ball is hit, it strikes an object ball, creating a chain reaction that can involve many interactions between the balls on the table. Just as you exist in life, you encounter many phenomena that can lead you down many different paths. Life unfolds this way, ever changing and filled with many situations and options. We try to fulfill our wishes, but the outcome may fall short of our desires and expectations. Often this results in frustration, anger, and unhappiness. The root cause of this disintegrated nature is not the undesired outcome, but how we interpret it in our *conscious mind*.

The Conscious Mind

The mind performs a number of functions, including perceiving, feeling, making choices, and generating sensations associated within the awareness of the stated functions. From this awareness, choices are made, reasoning occurs, opinions are generated, preferences are stated, and judgments are formed. Life is measured and lived according to these formulations. The sensations of being happy, feeling free, excited, and liberated (to name a few) are by-products of some of your preferences and choices. These are sensations that feel good, and to some degree you'd like to replicate them often. In order to do that, you have to *abandon* a few things.

Fearless Abandon

I want to emphasize that all of this is taking place in your mind. All of it: the processing, deducing, figuring, and formulating. Keep that understanding on the front burner as you continue reading. OK, now that we have stroked the ego and given it the sense of security that it desires, we can safely strap ourselves in and continue on this fearless journey.

Abandon some beliefs and opinions. Do you identify yourself with a job title or your job? If you answered yes, this identification can be all encompassing, because it is how you define yourself. A professional athlete and a police officer are pretty strong examples. Asking an athlete to abandon seeing things through her sport, or a cop not to be a cop outside of work is hard, because that is how they see themselves. They also form opinions and beliefs according to their titles and roles.

Now this is huge. Some might even say it's impossible. This recommendation might stir up a lot of different feelings, because to suggest you let go of something that has been a large part of how you function, and even how you define yourself, is foreign and unusual. Forming opinions leads to manifesting them into beliefs. They become rooted, and from this, actions and relations sprout based on a series of these beliefs and opinions. This limits the potential for other experiences and inhibits the natural flow and your ability to just *be*. Your beliefs imply a philosophy of the mind that intentionally leads you into certain mental states and attitudes. These roads often lead to the same destinations.

In America, we have seen how beliefs manifest historically with slavery, lack of civil rights, women having no voting rights, the Salem witch trials, and currently with LGBT and gender equality, plus many other examples. This can lead to the creation of stereotypical responses and the minimization of a person due to ignorance and fear. Having ignorance by not understanding the subject or the experience, fearing the unknown aspects of it, and thinking it can potentially impact affect one's world negatively creates a limited thinking module.

Let's go back to the professional athlete and police officer to look at how their opinions and beliefs could manifest into their behaviors. If an officer is trained to react in order to keep or restore peace, he now believes that he is the authority to enforce this position in order for the outcome to be safe and placid. When the officer is off duty, chances are that he still believes he is the enforcer. If an athlete is off and not playing in any games, she still has a mentality of being in the best physical condition in order to perform. This can equate to the officer not fully engaging in activities freely, for he feels that he might have to act or maintain a stoic state in order to remain alert. The athlete may miss out on a seriously good and indulgent meal because she feels that it will hinder her future performance. The point here is that because of these beliefs, neither is fully engaged in their present moment. It keeps them from being immersed in the activity and flavors the moment is presenting.

These manifestations restricted the full potential of existence for the subjects within those situations. Having a rooted system of certain beliefs can restrict the full potential of your existence and is the very thing that restrains you from achieving happiness and satisfaction in your life on many levels. This limited perspective perpetuates a state of disintegration.

Without Opinion

What if you were to exist without opinions just for one day? It will probably be a difficult thing to do, but it could bring you a stillness and ease that you probably have never experienced before.

Let's say you are driving down the road and you see someone being cut off in another lane. The person who was just cut off begins to make gestures of anger, honking the horn and flipping off the offending driver. You are largely unaffected by this because it wasn't you who was cut off, and so you don't form an opinion about it. You continued on your merry way down the road, probably forgetting the whole thing before the next stoplight.

Now let's say that this driver cut **you** off instead! The whole game has changed now, right? Your **opinion** steps in, and out of your mouth fly all kinds of things directed at the driver, and you throw in a few honks on the horn. It's safe to say that this is not a stilling, ease-filled feeling, right?

Now let's rewind to you being the witness and driving down the road on your merry way—can you detect a peace and ease about the situation then? Probably so, because your opinion was removed and you weren't personally involved.

The detachment existed for the non-personal situation, and therefore the mind had no fluctuation.

This is just one example of how the removal of opinion can create stillness. Obtaining freedom and an unconditional existence occurs when you become integrated into the constant stream of "is-ness" and the Now. This begins with taming and suppressing the mind.

Practice Makes Stillness

Once a conscious effort is made to control the fluctuations of the mind, aspects of your steady state will be revealed. Over time, this is the state that you will exist in.

Applying this practice can be done as a test first, just to see what you're working with. When the next opportunity arises for you to insert your opinion, stop, take a breath, and begin to witness the situation from a "seer's" perspective. Become a witness to how things are, how they unfold, and most important, witness how you *are* as this is occurring. Do you feel the need to speak up? What are your thoughts? Do you feel relieved or indifferent to this detachment?

As this self-study is happening, you are practicing restraining the modifications of the mind. Taking a pause from action to become aware and in the moment trains the mind to be still.

Stilling the mind so that your thoughts can align with ease and peace is a discipline that takes practice and commitment, and it can seem like a task rather than enjoyment. Most things that involve discipline are viewed as difficult or not enjoyable, so people don't want to do them. If that could potentially happen to you, consider this: What if you were to view this so it wouldn't be such a task? First, keep on your front burner the state of mind that you want to be in, and the purpose of it. Then know that when you apply this practice, the situations will be different and you'll get a new perspective. That alone is refreshing, because the phenomenon that exists in every situation changes with every interaction. Perhaps your viewpoint will shift to seeing the application as exciting instead of task-filled, Because of the ever-changing landscape, you have an ongoing opportunity to experience things differently every time you apply this practice.

Try not to formulate an instant opinion or lock yourself into a mode when a situation arises. Instead, experiment as life happens, see and study how you are within situations. These are all opportunities to apply the discipline of taming and suppressing the mind. This practice can be applied in most situations. Take a fearless approach toward shifting the paradigm that you exist within.

What Do You Believe?

Let's talk about beliefs for a moment. When you believe something, you root yourself in it. This limits the potential for other experiences and inhibits the natural flow, therefore limiting your ability to just be. Your beliefs imply a philosophy of the mind that intentionally leads you into certain mental states and attitudes. These roads often lead to the same destinations all the time because you never take a different route.

The moment you categorize and put things into boxes, you limit the process of expansive, limitless thought.

Creativity is powerful, and it is constant. Being creative allows you to be connected to the flow of life, experiencing new facets, seeing the unconditional nature of your true self through the eyes of the non-opinionated, non-judgmental witness.

Shedding the Layers

By allowance and experimentation, you can begin shedding the many layers of *beliefs, opinions,* and distractions that limit the creativity, awareness, and natural flow of what resides within. This can and will ultimately lead you to the true understanding of how your mind has been limiting the happy and true existence that is already occurring within you.

When you are still, you can then see!

It's a Wrap!
Final Thoughts

~

As we traverse this thing called life, we are faced with challenges, opportunities, and choices. It is part of our personal evolution to become aware of our needs and how we are living life. Sometimes it's not an obvious thought that leads us to this awareness. Situations, circumstances, people we meet, or just living day to day may bring us exactly where we need to be in order to have a front-row seat to see clearly what our needs truly are.

Having this information is one thing; doing something with it is another. There are a lot of reasons why you would not choose to activate this awareness and make changes to shift your life. It could be inconvenient timing-wise or cause a disruption within your current life pattern. It even could be fear of the unknown. All of these reasons are valid and real; however, you should look at them honestly and objectively to see if there is any room for consideration and change. What people regret most as they look back on their lives is that they wished they had lived a life that was true to themselves and they wish they lived a lot happier life than they did. For me personally, I often think about these regrets, and I don't want them to be mine. So in hope of transforming any future regrets before they manifest, this book was created to inspire you to live a full, true, and happy life while you're here and fully able to enjoy it!

Have at it, my friend.

Personal Notes

_____

_____

_____

_____

_____

_____

_____

_____

_____

_____

CPSIA information can be obtained
at www.ICGtesting.com
Printed in the USA
FSOW04n1146140616
21488FS